{IT CHANGED THE WORLD}

INVENTION OF SPACE EXPLORATION

Mike Downs

ROURKE'S SCHOOL to HOME CONNECTIONS

BEFORE AND DURING READING ACTIVITIES

Before Reading: *Building Background Knowledge and Vocabulary*

Building background knowledge can help children process new information and build upon what they already know. Before reading a book, it is important to tap into what children already know about the topic. This will help them develop their vocabulary and increase their reading comprehension.

Questions and Activities to Build Background Knowledge:

1. Look at the front cover of the book and read the title. What do you think this book will be about?
2. What do you already know about this topic?
3. Take a book walk and skim the pages. Look at the table of contents, photographs, captions, and bold words. Did these text features give you any information or predictions about what you will read in this book?

Vocabulary: *Vocabulary Is Key to Reading Comprehension*

Use the following directions to prompt a conversation about each word.

- Read the vocabulary words.
- What comes to mind when you see each word?
- What do you think each word means?

Vocabulary Words:
- asteroids
- atmosphere
- galaxies
- optical telescopes
- orbit
- rockets
- rovers
- satellites
- spacecraft
- wavelengths

During Reading: *Reading for Meaning and Understanding*

To achieve deep comprehension of a book, children are encouraged to use close reading strategies. During reading, it is important to have children stop and make connections. These connections result in deeper analysis and understanding of a book.

Close Reading a Text

During reading, have children stop and talk about the following:

- Any confusing parts
- Any unknown words
- Text to text, text to self, text to world connections
- The main idea in each chapter or heading

Encourage children to use context clues to determine the meaning of any unknown words. These strategies will help children learn to analyze the text more thoroughly as they read.

When you are finished reading this book, turn to the next-to-last page for **Text-Dependent Questions** and an **Extension Activity**.

TABLE OF CONTENTS

Race to Space 4
To the Moon 8
Satellites and Telescopes 12
Probes and Discoveries 19
Astronauts and Tourists 26
Glossary 30
Index 31
Text-Dependent Questions 31
Extension Activity 31
About the Author 32

RACE TO SPACE

Before people began exploring space, scientists could only guess what the moon was made of. People joked that it might be green cheese!

Nobody really believed that, but they couldn't prove it was wrong. The best way to find out what made up the moon and everything else in the night sky was to go there and see for ourselves.

IMPORTANT SPACE BEGINNINGS

When you think of space, you might think of the National Aeronautics and Space Administration (NASA). This part of the United States government encourages the peaceful use of space programs. It began in 1958.

In the 1940s, World War II was ending. The rush for space flight, called the *Space Race*, began. The United States and the United Soviet Socialist Republic, also called the Soviet Union, each wanted to be first in space. **Rockets** were new at this time, though many of them failed and exploded soon after takeoff.

As rockets got more reliable, people prepared to put astronauts in space. The earliest space travelers were not human. They were fruit flies, mice, monkeys, dogs, a rabbit, and a cat.

Yuri Gagarin was the first person in space. His mission launched on April 12, 1961, in the Soviet Union's *Vostok 1* **spacecraft**. The flight lasted 108 minutes.

Gagarin's flight went around Earth one time before the spacecraft returned to ground level.

TO THE MOON

At the time of Gagarin's flight, technology was limited. Desktop computers and handheld calculators had not yet been invented. Much of the math needed for early space exploration was done by people rather than by machines. Computers back then were so large that they sometimes filled entire rooms. They would stop working or turn off suddenly. Some astronauts did not like trusting these early computers with their lives.

It took scientists such as Dr. Katherine Johnson and Annie Easley to make space exploration possible. They did the math necessary for launching spacecraft. Later, when computers became more powerful, they worked on the launching and tracking of rockets and other space technology.

Annie Easley's work is still used to develop technology.

Large computers such as this one were among the first to be used in space exploration.

Early space flight was dangerous. Parachutes often failed, and spacecraft fell apart during or shortly after launch. Testing was necessary but often dangerous. Many astronauts were injured or died.

Dr. Katherine Johnson

SOLVING SCIENTIFIC PUZZLES

When problems happen, you can sometimes understand what caused them by studying the end result. Part of the work that Dr. Katherine Johnson did was analyzing data from failed test flights and crashes. This information helped scientists improve spacecraft and make space technology safer.

Despite the danger, scientists kept trying to launch people safely into space. On July 20, 1969, a United States spacecraft carrying a crew of three landed on the moon. Neil Armstrong and Buzz Aldrin were the first astronauts to walk on the moon.

Buzz Aldrin salutes the U.S. flag on the moon.

SATELLITES AND TELESCOPES

Putting people on the moon was only part of the Space Race. Around the same time, countries began launching **satellites** without any people on them. Satellites could gather lots of information without putting astronauts in danger. Early satellites were used for communication, spying, and studying weather. Modern satellites can do much more!

Some satellites travel at the same speed as Earth. This helps them work better.

Some satellites study planets, stars, and **asteroids**. Others measure light and radio energy. NASA's Solar Dynamics Observatory satellite studies our sun. Satellites map the world. They transmit hundreds of television channels. They send global positioning signals to show your location. Satellites are part of our everyday lives.

Thousands of satellites now **orbit** Earth. Some are as large as buses. Others are smaller than coffee cups. KalamSat is a satellite designed by high school students from India. It is so small that it could fit in the palm of your hand.

This photo of a coast in South America was taken with satellites. It shows light from things such as cities, wildfires, and fishing boats. Some major satellites are shown at right.

14

CRIME-STOPPING SATELLITES

Illegal fishing can be monitored and stopped when satellites track the movement of boats across the water. A computer can let scientists know when a boat has stayed in one place too long and might be fishing.

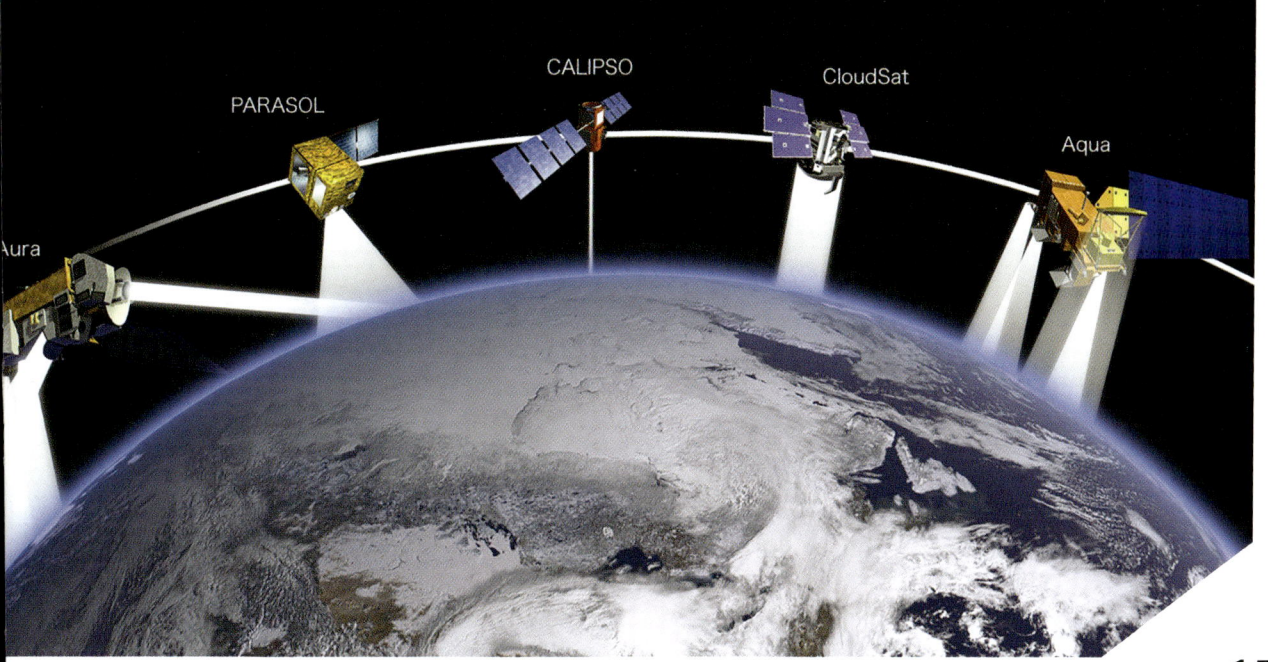

15

Space exploration can be done from Earth with satellites and other technology, but Earth's **atmosphere** distorts the picture we see. **Optical telescopes** are a solution to this problem. The best ones are built high on mountains. This keeps them above most clouds and in clear air.

Radio telescopes are important for space exploration. They detect radio energy emitted from planets, stars, and gases in outer space. The atmosphere doesn't bother radio telescopes. They can detect many things that optical telescopes can't.

BIGGER IS BETTER

The world's largest optical telescope is being built in Chile. It has a mirror diameter of 128 feet (39 meters). China has the largest radio telescope, with a dish diameter of 1,640 feet (500 meters).

The life-sized James Webb Space Telescope model sits in front of the Royal Hospital Kilmainham in Dublin, Ireland.

17

Telescopes can also be sent into space. The Hubble Space Telescope is a satellite. It provides incredible photos of exploding stars and newly forming **galaxies**. The newer and larger James Webb Space Telescope can provide even more impressive photos.

The Milky Way galaxy is named this way because it looks like milk in the sky.

DUSTY GALAXY

The beautiful night view of our Milky Way galaxy is not the whole picture. The dark sections we see are clouds of space dust that block our view. Radio telescopes are not affected by the dust.

18

PROBES AND DISCOVERIES

Satellites aren't the only things shot into space. Hundreds of research vehicles without passengers, called space probes, have also been launched. Space probes are sent out to study planets, asteroids, comets, the sun, and space itself.

19

Several probes have been sent to Mars. A few included land **rovers** that moved across the planet. Unfortunately, a massive dust storm covered Mars in June 2018. It caused the failure of the rover *Opportunity*, which had successfully sent data since 2004. Another rover, *Curiosity*, survived the storm.

Probes can spend years collecting data. The information from these probes can be used by scientists to create and improve technology.

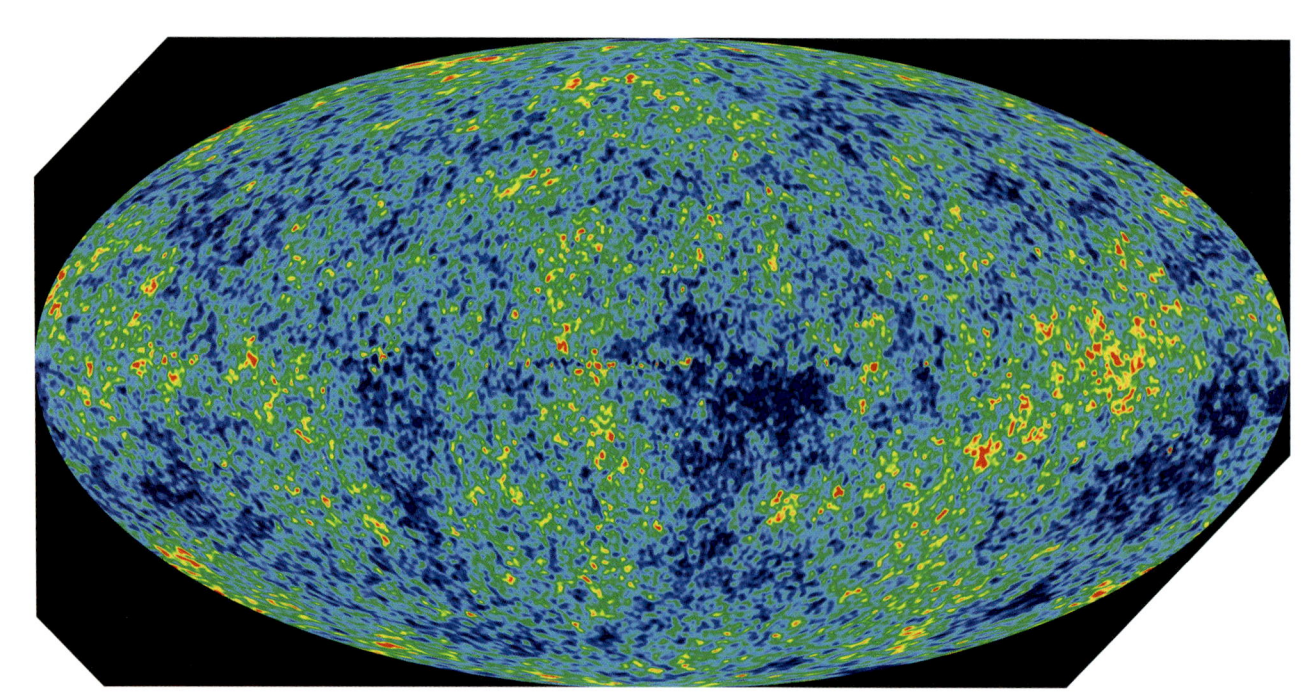

The Wilkinson Microwave Anisotropy Probe (WMAP) was a spacecraft used to measure temperature differences across the sky. The WMAP was used to take this photo. The red regions are warm, and the blue regions are cold.

NASA's Curiosity rover took this selfie on Mars.

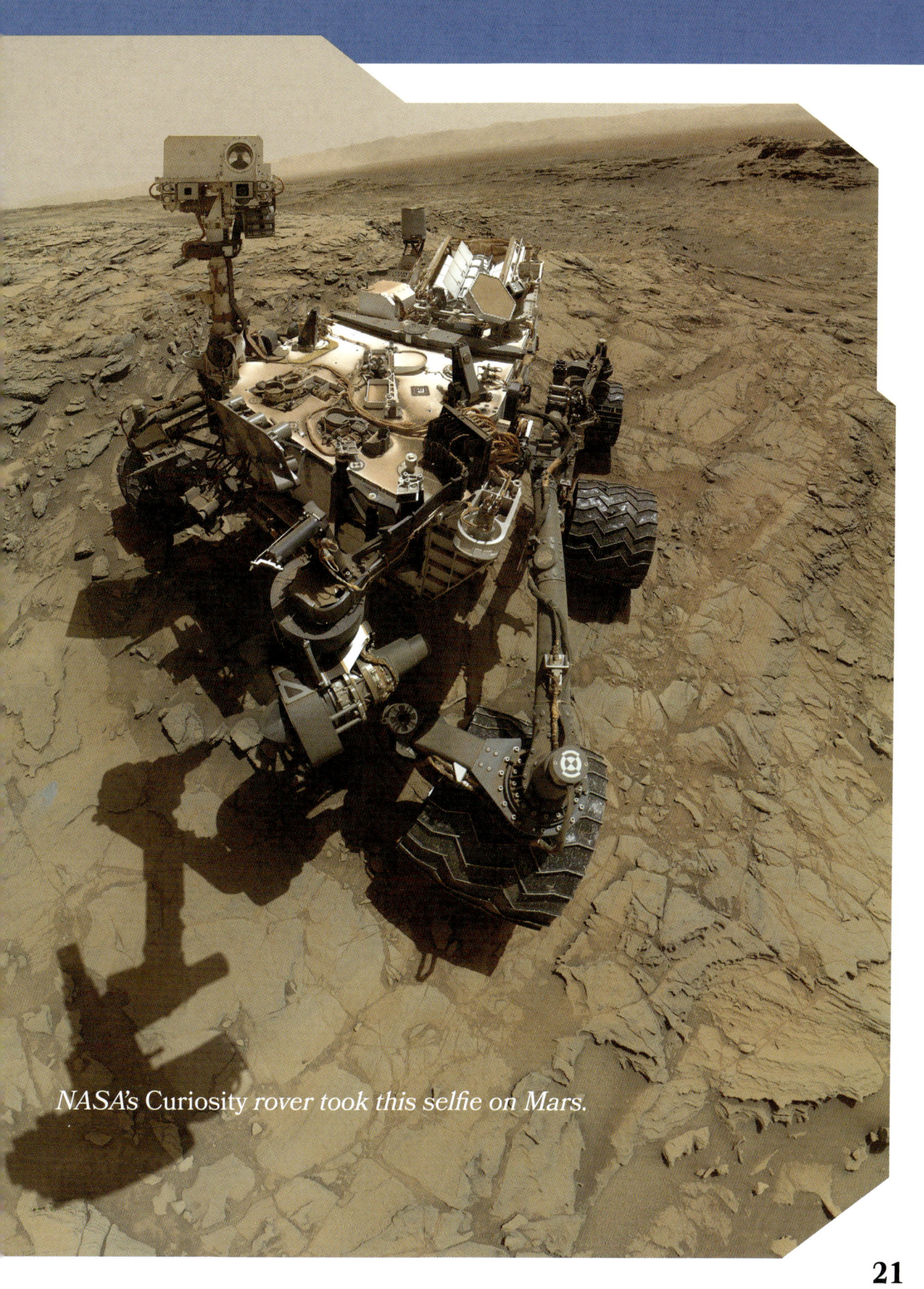

Using space exploration technology, scientists recently found a galaxy that is 13.4 billion years old. That means it formed only 400 million years after the universe as we know it was first formed. The beginning of the universe is referred to as the *Big Bang*.

Wavelengths and Energy

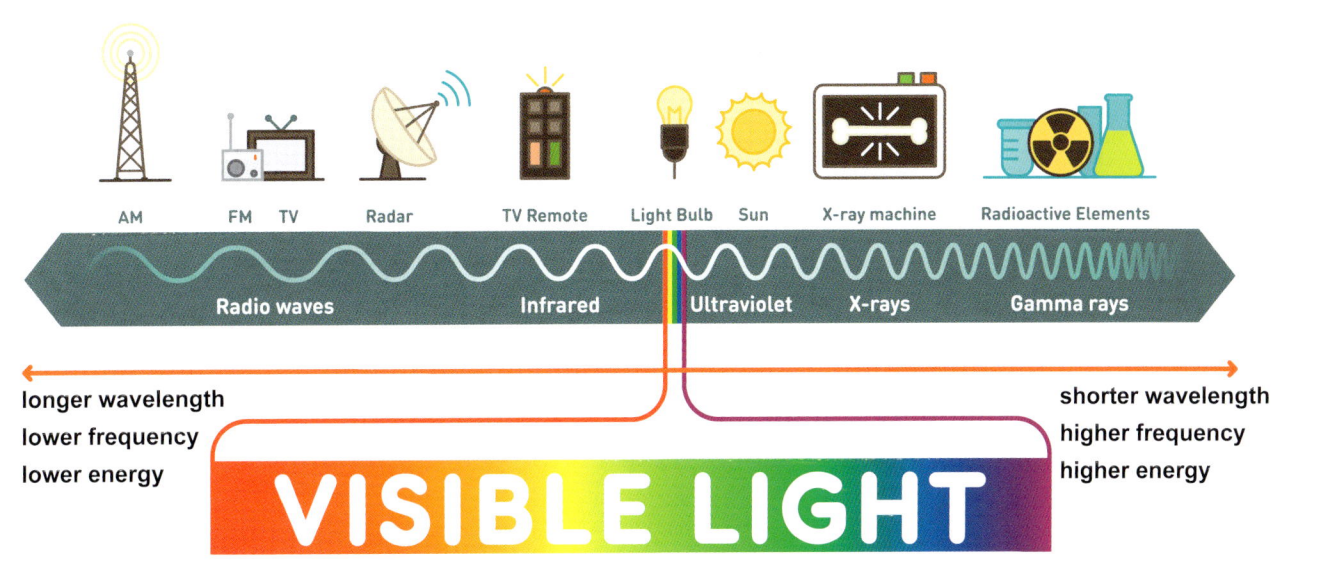

AM	FM TV	Radar	TV Remote	Light Bulb	Sun	X-ray machine	Radioactive Elements

Radio waves | Infrared | Ultraviolet | X-rays | Gamma rays

longer wavelength
lower frequency
lower energy

shorter wavelength
higher frequency
higher energy

VISIBLE LIGHT

Other studies showed that the universe is growing larger. Scientists discovered this by measuring the **wavelengths** of light.

Light, heat, and radio energy moves in wave shapes. They move too fast to see. You can tell the kind of waves apart by looking at their shapes and wavelengths. Changes in wavelength also give us information. An object moving away will have a shift in the wavelength of light. Scientists have discovered many such shifts when studying space.

Space exploration has also led to technological discoveries and advances. It helped with the invention of cordless vacuum cleaners and thermometers that go into ears. Thanks to space research, we can harness the sun's power. We even have better baby food and special sunglasses based on designs used for space travel!

Space technology can be used to scan for transmissions from outer space. It might even help us find life on another planet one day.

ASTRONAUTS AND TOURISTS

Astronauts conduct many types of experiments, mostly on space stations. They are learning what effect space has on people, animals, and plants. This helps scientists prepare for future journeys in space.

There have been about 13 space stations. The *International Space Station* is still in flight and has had full-time crews since 2001.

Other space station missions are planned for the near future. Both China and the United States are planning missions to Mars in the next decade that will carry people. One lucky astronaut will be the first to step onto the planet!

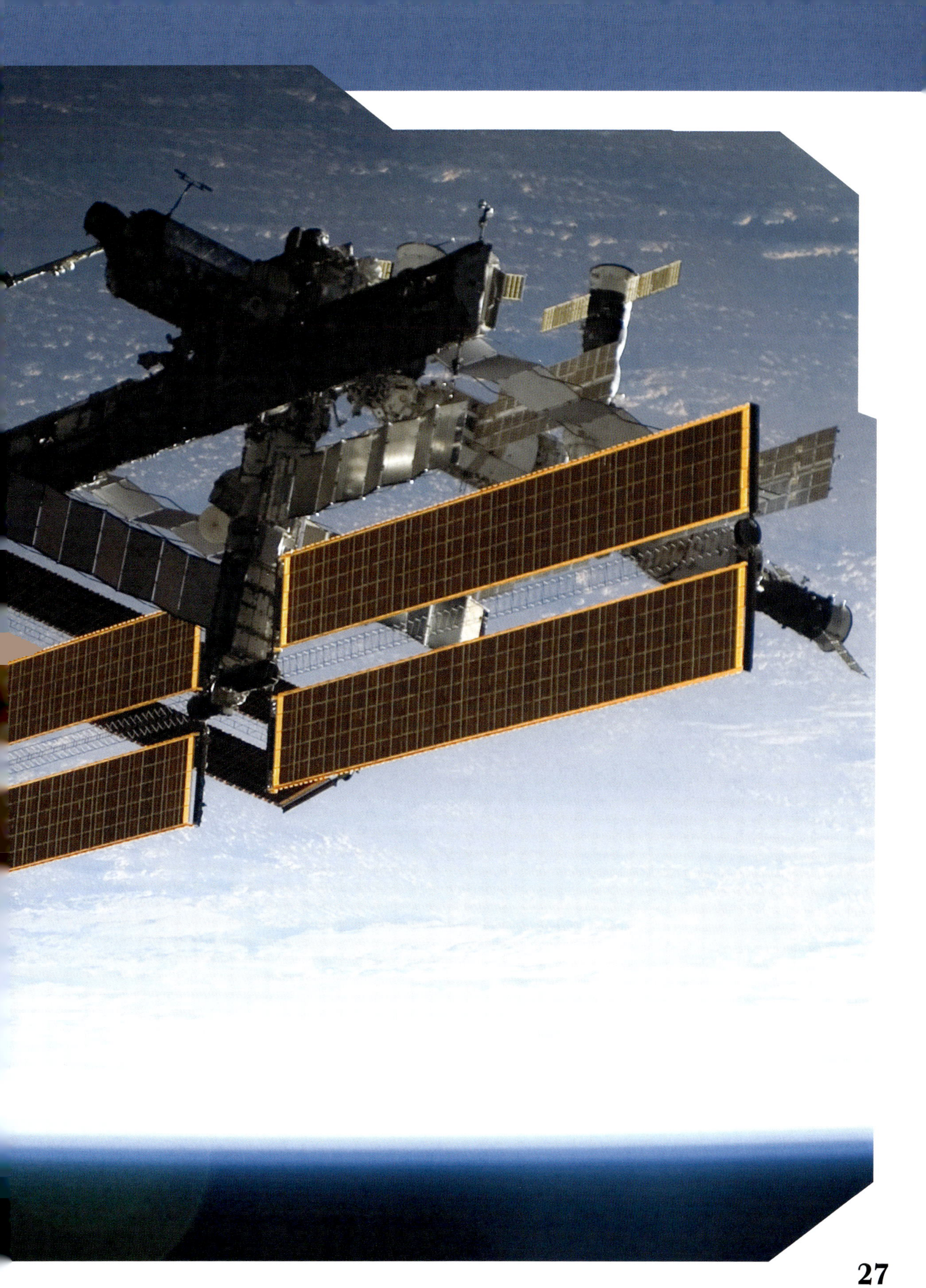

With all of the advancements in space exploration, it is possible that people who are not astronauts might visit other planets one day. Some people imagine building places for lots of people to live on Mars or other planets. Others dream of visiting another planet for a vacation. Where would you like to travel in space?

This drawing shows what life on Mars might look like.

28

Even though space exploration happens a long way from Earth, it has led to huge changes here. We have developed much better technology because of space research. We know much more about the universe. We are learning what it might take for humans to live on other planets. Space exploration has definitely changed the world. How will it change your life?

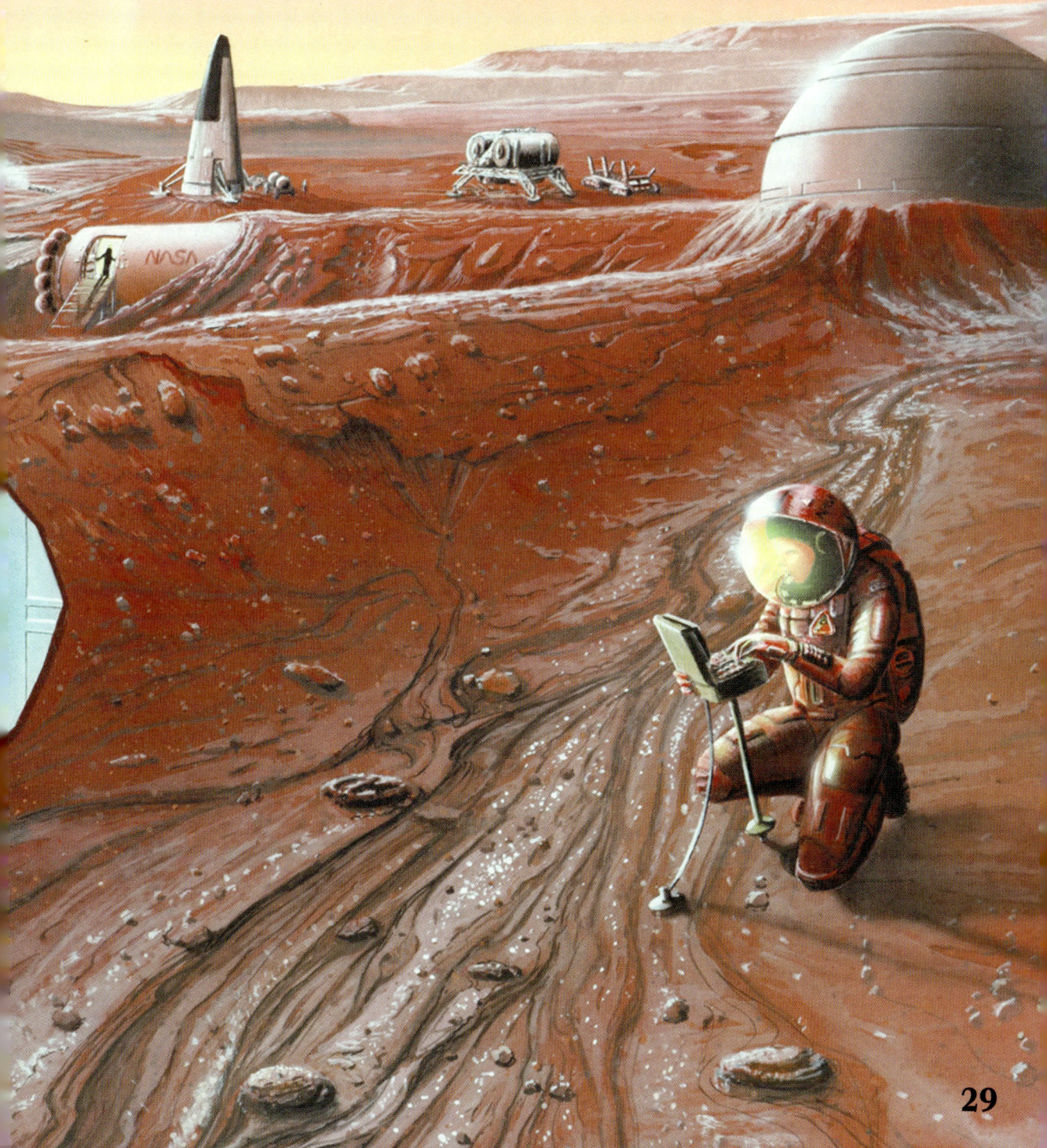

GLOSSARY

asteroids (AS-tuh-roids): objects, smaller than planets, that orbit the sun

atmosphere (AT-muhs-feer): the gases, mostly oxygen and nitrogen, that surround Earth

galaxies (GAL-uhk-seez): groups of millions or billions of stars

optical telescopes (AHP-ti-kuhl TEL-uh-skopes): telescopes that gather and focus light to create an enlarged image

orbit (OR-bit): travel a curved path around a planet or star

rockets (RAH-kehts): vehicles that are pushed into the air at a high speed with an engine that burns high-power fuel

rovers (ROH-vurz): robots that travel on the surface of planets, moons, or asteroids

satellites (SAT-uh-lites): objects that orbit around planets or stars

spacecraft (SPAYSE-kraft): a vehicle or machine designed for flight or other work in space

wavelengths (WAYV-lengkths): distances between waves, such as light waves

INDEX

Easley, Annie 8
Gagarin, Yuri 6, 7, 8
Hubble Space Telescope 18
International Space Station 26
Johnson, Katherine 8, 10

Mars 20, 21, 26, 28
moon landing 11
Space Race 5, 12
telescopes 16, 17, 18
universe 22, 23, 29

TEXT-DEPENDENT QUESTIONS

1. How are scientists able to study outer space?
2. Why is it important to make bigger and better telescopes?
3. What are some things satellites can do?
4. What are two different types of telescopes?
5. What planet has had several rovers on it?

EXTENSION ACTIVITY

The Search for Extraterrestrial Intelligence (SETI) Institute searches for signs of alien life. Create a message you would send to an alien civilization on a distant planet. Be sure to consider the material you use as well as the message itself.

ABOUT THE AUTHOR

Mike Downs loves to fly! He has flown fighters, airliners, hang gliders, and tow-planes. He hopes to fly as a space tourist too! Mike also loves to write. When he's not off on an adventure, he's busy writing books.

© 2020 Rourke Educational Media

All rights reserved. No part of this book may be reproduced or utilized in any form or by any means, electronic or mechanical including photocopying, recording, or by any information storage and retrieval system without permission in writing from the publisher.

www.rourkeeducationalmedia.com

PHOTO CREDIT: Cover, pages 4, 5, 6, 8, 9, 10, 11, 12-13, 14, 15, 26-27, 28-29: ©NASA; page 7: ©akg-images; page 15b: ©Steve Froebe; pages 16-17: ©Richard Bent; pages 18, 21: ©NASA/JPL-Caltech; page 22: ©Korn V.; page 24a: ©scanrail; page 24b: ©cerro_photography; page 24c: ©jevtic; page 25: ©Sharply_done

Edited by: Tracie Santos
Cover and interior layout by: Kathy Walsh

Library of Congress PCN Data

Invention of Space Exploration / Mike Downs
(It Changed the World)
ISBN 978-1-73162-980-7 (hard cover)(alk. paper)
ISBN 978-1-73162-974-6 (soft cover)
ISBN 978-1-73162-986-9 (e-Book)
ISBN 978-1-73163-333-0 (ePub)
Library of Congress Control Number: 2019945501

Rourke Educational Media
Printed in the United States of America,
North Mankato, Minnesota